GATE

The Gate Theatre presents

The UK Premiere of

NOCTURNAL

BY JUAN MAYORGA

TRANSLATED BY DAVID JOHNSTON

First performed in English in the UK
at the Gate Theatre, London on 16 April 2009

The translation of this play was originally commissioned by the Royal Court Theatre

GW00481258

Significant Annual Support from

NOCTURNAL
BY JUAN MAYORGA

TRANSLATED BY DAVID JOHNSTON

Cast (in alphabetical order)

Doctor	**Matthew Dunster**
Short Man	**Paul Hunter**
Short Woman	**Amanda Lawrence**
Tall Woman	**Justine Mitchell**
Tall Man	**Justin Salinger**

Director	**Lyndsey Turner**
Designers	**Matthew Walker & Hannah Clark**
Animator	**Matthew Walker**
Lighting Designer	**Katharine Williams**
Sound Designer	**Christopher Shutt**
Assistant Director	**Freya Elliott**
Props Supervisor	**Joe Schermoly**

Production Manager	**Marius Rønning**
Stage Manager	**Charlotte Padgham**
AV Consultant	**Ian Galloway**
Technical Production Assistant	**Joe Schermoly**
Production Electrician	**Chris Porter**
Assistant Stage Manager Intern	**Rachel Jacobs**

Casting	**Lucy Bevan**
Press	**Clióna Roberts for CRPR** **(cliona@crpr.co.uk | 07754 756504)**
Production Photographer	**Catherine Ashmore**

The Gate would like to thank the following people for their help with this production: AKA, Nicola Biden, Big Wheel Theatre, Sorcha Cusack, Elyse Dodgson, Georgia Fitch, Gate Restaurant, Hampstead Theatre, Jan Haydn Rowles, Gerard Horan, Mark Goddard, D C Jackson, Chris James, Ruth Little, Miles Mantle, Duncan MacMillan, David McSeveney, Mesmer, Ruth Murfitt, National Theatre, Orlando Reade, Russell Tovey, Luke Swaffield, Will at Factory Settings.

Special thanks to **Simon Breden**

Production Image © **Todd M Hall**

Biographies

Lucy Bevan **Casting**

For the Gate credits include: *State of Emergency, Hedda, The Internationalist, I Am Falling, The Car Cemetery, The Sexual Neuroses of Our Parents.* Other theatre includes: *Camera Obscura* (Almeida); *The Boy Who Fell Into a Book* (English Touring Theatre). Film includes: *An Education, Nanny McPhee and the Big Bang, Me and Orson Welles, The Duchess, The Golden Compass, St. Trinians, The Last Legion, Chromophobia, The Libertine.*

Hannah Clark **Designer**

For the Gate credits include: *Big Love.* Other theatre includes: *Billy Wonderful* (Liverpool Everyman); *The Snow Queen* (West Yorkshire Playhouse); *Proper Clever* (Liverpool Playhouse); *Pequenas Delicias* (Requardt & Co); *Torn* (Arcola); *Roadkill Café* (Requardt & Co, The Place); *House of Agnes* (Paines Plough); *Breakfast with Mugabe* (Theatre Royal Bath – Ustinov); *The Cracks in My Skin* (Manchester Royal Exchange Studio); *Othello* (Salisbury Playhouse); *Who's Afraid of Virginia Woolf?* (Manchester Royal Exchange); *Terre Haute* (Assembly Rooms/Trafalgar Studio 2/UK Tour/59E59 Theaters, New York); *Jammy Dodgers* (Requardt & Co, The Place/Royal Opera House 2); *The Taming of The Shrew* (Bristol Old Vic).

Matthew Dunster **Doctor**

Theatre includes: *The Daughter in Law* (Young Vic); *Toast, Plasticine, Under the Whaleback, Harvest* (Royal Court); The Permanent Way (National Theatre/Out of Joint). As a director, credits include: *Macbeth* (Manchester Royal Exchange); *You Can See the Hills, Love and Money* (Manchester Royal Exchange/Young Vic); *Frontline* (Globe); *Testing the Echo* (Out of Joint); *The Member of the Wedding* (Young Vic). As a writer for the stage, credits include: *You Can See the Hills* (Manchester Royal Exchange/Young Vic); *You Used To* (Contact); *Tell Me* (Contact/Donmar); *Two Clouds Over Eden* (Manchester Royal Exchange). Matthew is an Associate Director of the Young Vic.

Freya Elliott **Assistant Director**

Freya gained an MA in Visual Media for Performance at Central School of Speech of Drama, a BA in Fine Art at Oxford University, and last year trained at the London International School of Performing Arts. As an artist and director she makes films, multimedia installations and digital performances. After her MA Freya was selected to exhibit in Saatchi's *4 New Sensations* Exhibition, and has made work at the ICA, BAC, and Barbican Art Gallery.

Ian Galloway **AV Consultant**

Ian is a video designer, director and programmer, and has worked with visuals since graduating from Rose Bruford College. His design and assistant design credits include: *Measure for Measure, A Minute Too Late* (Complicite); *Proper Clever* (Liverpool Playhouse); *Baby Girl, DNA, The Miracle* (National Theatre); *Blood* (Royal Court); *Hitchcock Blonde* (Alley Theater, Houston). He works as part of the creative collective Mesmer.

Paul Hunter **Short Man**

Theatre includes: *A Midsummer Night's Dream, Under the Black Flag* (Globe); *Rapunzel* (Kneehigh/BAC/New York); *The Play What I Wrote* (West End); *The Water Engine* (Young Vic/Theatre503); *Oliver Twist, Aladdin, Pinocchio* (Lyric Hammersmith); *Playing the Victim* (Traverse/Royal Court); *I Can't Wake Up, Happy Birthday, Mister Deka D, Don't Laugh – It's My Life* (Told By An Idiot); *The Red Shoes* (Kneehigh); *Les Enfants du Paradis* (RSC). Television includes: *Black Books, Trinity, After You're Gone, Absolute Power.* As a director, credits include: *The Comedy of Errors* (RSC/Told By An Idiot); *Señora Carrar's Rifles* (Young Vic); *Beauty and The Beast, Casanova* (Told By An Idiot/Lyric Hammersmith). Paul is a co-founder of Told By An Idiot theatre company.

Rachel Jacobs
Assistant Stage Manager Intern

Rachel studied a BA in Dramatic Arts at University of Witwatersrand, Johannesburg, where she gained experience of stage management, directing and acting. Credits include: *Le Carnival de ma Vie* (Stage Manager); *CBeebies Live!* (Arena Tour 2006). Rachel is excited to be working at the Gate.

David Johnston **Translator**

David is Professor of Hispanic Studies and Head of the School of Languages, Literatures and Performing Arts at Queen's University, Belfast. He is an award-winning translator for the stage, and has translated over thirty plays from Spanish, Portuguese and French. He was heavily involved in the Gate Theatre's *Spanish Golden Age* season 1992/93; and has been commissioned by the Royal Shakespeare Company (including Lope de Vega's *The Dog in the Manger*); the Royal Court (including their Mexican season *Arena Mexico*) and by BBC television and radio. With Catherine Boyle and Jonathan Thacker, he co-directs Out of the Wings (www.outofthewings.org.uk), an AHRC-funded Spanish theatre translation project.

Amanda Lawrence **Short Woman**

Theatre includes: *Purgatory* (Arcola); *Brief Encounter* (Birmingham Rep/Kneehigh); *Cymbeline*, *The Wooden Frock* (Kneehigh); *Nights at the Circus* (Lyric Hammersmith/ Kneehigh); *Tristan & Yseult* (National Theatre/Kneehigh); *The Fireworks Maker's Daughter* (Told By An Idiot/Lyric Hammersmith); *Playing the Victim* (Royal Court/Told By An Idiot); *Grimm Tales*, *More Grimm Tales*, *Animal Farm* (Northern Stage). Television includes: *The Well*, *Above Suspicion*, *Afterlife*, *Clone*, *Little Dorrit*, *Little Miss Jocelyn*, *Doctor Who*, *Hotel Babylon*. Film includes: *Womb*, *Me Me Me*, *Hard Told*, *28 Weeks Later*.

Juan Mayorga **Writer**

Juan was born in Madrid in 1965. Plays include: *El traductor de Blumemberg*, *El jardín quemado*, *Cartas de amor a Stalin*, *El Gordo y el Flaco*, *Himmelweg*, *Últimas palabras de Copito de Nieve*, *Hamelin*, *El chico de la última fila*, *La tortuga de Darwin* and *La paz perpetua*. *Himmelweg* has been performed under the title *Way to Heaven* at the Royal Court and by Galloglass Company. English translations

of his work have been published in the UK: *The Scorched Garden* (*El jardín quemado*) and in USA: *Love Letters to Stalin* (*Cartas de amor a Stalin*). His work has been premiered in eighteen countries, translated into sixteen languages, and he has written versions of plays by other playwrights including Shakespeare, Lessing, Ibsen and Chekhov.

Justine Mitchell **Tall Woman**

Theatre includes: *The Stone* (Royal Court); *Hedda Gabler*, *Footfalls*, *Pride and Prejudice*, *Blithe Spirit*, *bash* (Gate Theatre, Dublin); *Three Sisters*, *Aristocrats*, *The Shape of Metal*, *She Stoops to Conquer*, *The House of Bernarda Alba* (Abbey Theatre, Dublin); *The Hour We Knew Nothing of Each Other*, *Philistines*, *Coram Boy*, *The House of Bernarda Alba*, *The Night Season* (National Theatre); *Twelfth Night* (RSC). Television includes: *Your Bad Self*, *Sleep with Me*, *Waking the Dead*, *Afterlife*, *New Tricks*. Film includes: *A Cock and Bull Story*, *Inside I'm Dancing*, *Imagine Me and You*.

Charlotte Padgham **Stage Manager**

Theatre includes, as Deputy Stage Manager: *Complicit*, *Speed-the-Plow*, *All About My Mother*, *The Entertainer* (Old Vic); *Aristo* (Chichester Festival Theatre); *The Winterling*, *My Name is Rachel Corrie* (Royal Court); five years touring with Shared Experience. As Stage Manager, credits include: *The Lesson* (Arcola); *Rough Cuts: Midnight Revolutions* and *Chronic*, *Catch*, *On Insomnia and Midnight* (Royal Court). Charlotte is also a mentor, visiting professional and lecturer at Central School of Speech and Drama.

Marius Rønning **Production Manager**

Marius graduated from RADA in 2001 where he trained in Stage Management and Technical Theatre and since then he has been working on a freelance basis. He has worked for Tête à Tête Opera since 2001 and is currently the Technical Director for Tête à Tête's Opera Festival. Other companies include: Trestle (Mask), Royal College of Music, New Kent Opera, English Touring Opera, Wee (Dance), The Shout, Actors Touring Company, Soho

Theatre Company, Arcola Theatre, Royal Court, Hampstead Theatre and Grange Park Opera.

Justin Salinger **Tall Man**

For the Gate credits include: *Candide*. Other theatre includes: *Dealer's Choice* (original production), *The Seagull*, *A Dream Play*, *Pillars of the Community*, *The UN Inspector*, *Iphigenia at Aulis*, *Chips with Everything*, *Peter Pan* (National Theatre); *King of Hearts* (Out of Joint); *Bliss*, *Food Chain*, *Under the Blue Sky* (Royal Court); *The Birthday Party* (Lyric Hammersmith); *The Unthinkable*, *Kick for Touch* (Sheffield Crucible); *Privates on Parade* (Donmar); *Much Ado About Nothing* (Cheek By Jowl). Television includes: *Whistleblowers*, *He Kills Coppers*, *New Tricks*, *The Line of Beauty*. Film includes: *Daylight Robbery*, *The Calling*, *Heartless*, *Creature*.

Joe Schermoly
Props Supervisor & Technical Production Assistant

Joe recently moved to London from Chicago where he studied Set Design and Art History at Northwestern University. For the Gate credits include: *Unbroken*. Work as a set designer and technician in Chicago theatre includes: *Richard III*, *The Constant Wife*, *The Mark of Zorro* and *The Aristocrats*.

Christopher Shutt **Sound Designer**

Theatre includes: *Burnt by the Sun*, *Every Good Boy Deserves Favour*, *Gethsemane*, *War Horse*, *Happy Days* (world tour), *Coram Boy*, *A Dream Play*, *Mourning Becomes Electra*, *Humble Boy*, *Play Without Words*, *Albert Speer*, *Not About Nightingales*, *Machinal* (National Theatre); *A Disappearing Number*, *The Elephant Vanishes*, *Mnemonic*, *The Street of Crocodiles*, *The Three Lives of Lucie Cabrol* (Complicite); *All My Sons*, *The Resistible Rise of Arturo Ui* (New York); *Bacchae*, *Little Otik* (National Theatre of Scotland); *A Moon for the Misbegotten*, *All About My Mother* (Old Vic); *Much Ado About Nothing*, *King John*, *Romeo and Juliet* (RSC); *Piaf*, *The Man Who Had All The Luck* (Donmar). Radio includes: *A Shropshire Lad*. Chris has received New York Drama Desk Awards for *Not About Nightingales* and *Mnemonic*. He has also received Olivier Award Nominations for *Coram Boy*, *War Horse* and *Piaf*.

Lyndsey Turner **Director**

Lyndsey is Associate Director of the Gate Theatre. As a director, credits include: *A Miracle*, *Contractions*, *Riot Boys*, *Chronic*, *Ignition* (Royal Court); *The Lesson* (Arcola); *Still Breathing*, *Hymn*, What's *Their Life Got?* (Theatre503); *The Grace of Mary Traverse* (LAMDA). As assistant director: *The City*, *Rhinoceros*, *The Vertical Hour*, *Krapp's Last Tape*, *Drunk Enough to Say I Love You*, *The Winterling* (Royal Court).

Matthew Walker
Designer & Animator

Matthew is an animator, writer and director based in Bristol. He is part of the animation company Arthur Cox Ltd and is represented as a commercials director with Aardman Animations. Since graduating from the University of Wales Newport in 2005 with his film *Astronauts*, Matthew has made three more short films (*John and Karen*, *Operator* and *Little Face*) as well as a variety of adverts and broadcast work. *Nocturnal* is his first experience of working on a theatre production.

Katharine Williams
Lighting Designer

Katharine is a lighting designer of drama, dance, physical theatre and opera, and creates dynamic, strong, image-driven work. She works in the UK and internationally, and her designs have been seen in China, Hong Kong, New Zealand, Canada, the USA, Mexico, Ireland, Holland, Spain, Italy, Germany, Armenia, Romania, Russia and the Czech Republic. For the Gate credits include: *Death and the Ploughman*, *The Sexual Neuroses of Our Parents*, *I Am Falling* (also Sadler's Wells, nominated for a South Bank Show Award), *Hedda*. Future projects include: *Underdrome* (Roundhouse, May 2009). Katharine was nominated for a 2008 Knight of Illumination Award for *I Am Falling*.

GATE

"The Gate is our oxygen. It should be on the National Health" *Bill Nighy*

The Gate, London's international theatre in the heart of Notting Hill, is renowned for its inventive use of space and the exceptional artists it attracts. An environment in which artists can create first-class and original theatre, the Gate is a springboard of opportunity, allowing emerging artists to excel and make their mark. With an average audience capacity of seventy, the space has challenged and inspired directors and designers for 30 years, making it famous for being one of the most flexible and transformable spaces in London.

"Great riches in a small space" *Sunday Times*

As joint Artistic Directors, Natalie Abrahami and Carrie Cracknell continue to create international work of the highest standard, which is peerless and provocative, and provides audiences with a unique experience.

"Under Natalie Abrahami and Carrie Cracknell this 70 seater theatre is suddenly out there in the vanguard of all that is exciting, explosive and invigorating in British Theatre. It has become a place of possibilities."
Lyn Gardner, The Guardian

Artistic Directors **Natalie Abrahami** and **Carrie Cracknell**
Producer **Jo Danvers**
General Manager **Undine Engelmann**
General Manager (Maternity Cover) **Kate Denby**
Production and Technical Manager **Nick Abbott**
Assistant Producer **Sam Sargant**
Production Assistant **Fiona Clift**
Community Projects Director **Lu Kemp**
Finance Assistant **Francis Makuwaza**
Intern **Matilda Long**
Duty Managers **Lavinia Hollands, Gina Peach**
Box Office **Alex Crampton, Adrian Figueroa, Leonie Kubigsteltig, Natalie Moukarzel, Louisa Sanfey**

Associate Director **Lyndsey Turner**
International Associates **Ugo Dehaes**, Pierre Rigal

The Gate Theatre Board of Trustees
Jonathan Hull (Chair), **Pim Baxter, Mark Bayley, Diane Borger, Natasha Bucknor, Rupert Christiansen, David Farr, Susan Hitch, Rima Horton** and **Colin Simon**

Development Associates **Cory Edelman Moss, Marianne Hinton**

Gate Theatre, 11 Pembridge Road, Notting Hill, London, W11 3HQ
www.gatetheatre.co.uk | Admin 020 7229 5387 | Box Office 020 7229 0706
The Gate Theatre Company is a company limited by guarantee. Registered in England & Wales No. 1495543
Charity No. 280278. Registered address: 11 Pembridge Road, Above the Price Albert Pub, London, W11 3HQ

SUPPORT THE **GATE**

We try to ensure that our creative ambitions are not bound by financial pressures; however, we rely on the generosity of our supporters for almost a third of our income in order to continue challenging form and breaking boundaries.

We need supporters who…

- **LOVE COMING TO THE GATE**
- **INTRODUCE THEIR FRIENDS TO THE GATE**
- **GIVE GENEROUSLY TO HELP THE GATE**

Supporters of the Gate receive benefits such as invitations to a host of events, including exclusive post-show drinks with cast and creative teams, a backstage glimpse of the running of the theatre, regular newsletters and priority booking. Supporters also have the opportunity to develop a close relationship with the Gate Theatre and the team who run it.

The very nature of our tiny venue means that you can see just how significant the support you give is to: our work, the nurturing of emerging talent and in bringing international theatre to London.

For more information on the Gate's work and how to support it, please visit www.gatetheatre.co.uk or contact Sam Sargant on 020 7229 5387 or sam@gatetheatre.co.uk.

The Gate Theatre would like to thank the following for their continued generous support:

Guardians Edward Field, Miles Morland, Jon and NoraLee Sedmak, Hilary and Stuart Williams, Anda and Bill Winters

Keepers Russ and Linda Carr, Lauren Clancy, Robert Devereux and Vanessa Branson, Cory Edelman Moss, David and Alexandra Emmerson, Leslie Feeney, Eric Fellner, Nick Ferguson, Marianne Hinton, Tony Mackintosh, Oberon Books, Elizabeth Price, David and Susie Sainsbury, The Ulrich Family

Lovers Anne Braillard, Kay Ellen Consolver and John Storkerson, Charles Cormick, James Fleming, Joachim Fleury, Bill and Stephanie Knight, David and Linda Lakhdhir, David Pike, Kerri Ratcliffe, Maurits Schouten, Kathryn Smith and Ike Udechuku, Tom Stoppard

Special thanks to Jenny Hall

Trusts & Foundations Anonymous, Arts Council England, Earls Court and Olympia Charitable Trust, The Eranda Foundation, Jerwood Charitable Foundation, The Mercers' Company, OAK Foundation, The Prince's Foundation for Children & the Arts, Royal Borough of Kensington and Chelsea

30 YEARS OF EXPLOSIVE INTERNATIONAL THEATRE 1979-2009

Courageous. Adventurous. Indomitable. Risk-taking. Spirited. Seminal. Renowned. All words that have been used to describe our much-loved theatre during the past thirty years.

In 1979 Lou Stein, an American theatrical entrepreneur with visionary ideas and a strong interest in European theatre and politics, applied for the lease of a run down studio over an equally run down ale house in bohemian Notting Hill. The Prince Albert's neighbours were artists, philosophers, writers and bums, perfect company for a burgeoning theatre with radical ideas.

The London Times reflected on the Gate's rapidly growing reputation:

"Lou Stein has transformed a room above a public house in Notting Hill into a theatre with a remarkable repertoire. In a space not much larger than a cupboard he has adapted and presented novels, and resurrected plays that have been grossly neglected elsewhere in Britain."

From the very first there was strong local support for the theatre – John Cleese gave the first donation of £10 towards Stein's work. We continue to have an army of loyal local supporters today, some of whom vividly remember the Lou Stein days.

In 1985 Stein handed over the reigns to Giles Croft and in 1990 the Gate became home to an ambitious young director by the name of Stephen Daldry, who cemented its reputation as a place of international tastes and talents. Between 1992 and 2007, the Gate was home to equally visionary artistic directors. Laurence Boswell, David Farr, Mick Gordon, Erica Whyman and Thea Sharrock each made a huge impact on the tiny space. Every one of these artists shared a delight in the freedom to fail and in the lightfootedness that comes with creating first class work on a shoestring. The Gate has won numerous awards and attracted many up-and-coming actors who have cut their teeth here and gone on to glittering careers.

Which brings us to 2009. As a venue which is continuously described as 'reinventing itself', as presenting 'new eras in theatre making' and 'launching careers of influential artists', 2009 will be a year for reflection and also a year for looking forward. A year for ensuring that the work presented by Natalie and Carrie continues in the indomitable spirit for which "London's most courageous theatre" is famous.

JO DANVERS PRODUCER

"THE GATE – STILL SWINGING AFTER 30 YEARS"
TOM STOPPARD

NOCTURNAL

First published in this translation in 2009 by Oberon Books Ltd
521 Caledonian Road, London N7 9RH
Tel: 020 7607 3637 / Fax: 020 7607 3629
e-mail: info@oberonbooks.com
www.oberonbooks.com

A catalogue record for this book is available from the British Library.

ISBN: 978-1-84002-923-9

Cover photograph by Todd M Hall

Printed in Great Britain by CPI Antony Rowe Ltd, Chippenham.

Contents

Introduction:
The Theatre of Juan Mayorga

Juan Mayorga (Madrid, 1965) is one of those exceptional writers who in every play seems to create theatre anew. The twenty or so full-length plays he has written to date all imagine the dynamics of the stage, and its endless relationships with an audience, in radically different and challenging ways: the cage in *Snowflake's Last Words* from which a dying albino gorilla delivers his final words of wisdom to the audience, cast as visitors to the zoo; a bare stage in *Hamelin* where the action, pared-back and Brechtian style, delivers a powerfully emotive re-casting of the legend of the Pied Piper; the compound of *Perpetual Peace* where a group of dogs, vying to join a crack security team, debate the morality of the western democracies' response to terrorism; the extended monologues and hypertheatricality of *Way to Heaven*, where the monstrosity of the Holocaust is reflected through the story of the camp at Theresienstadt; the process of psychological immersion that takes us into the fragile and increasingly delirious inner life of the writer Bulgakov who, in *Love Letters to Stalin*, pleads with the dictator to allow him to leave the Soviet Union; the bold denunciation of Spanish right-wing politics in *The Wedding of Ana and Alejandro,* performed in a Madrid restaurant specializing in wedding receptions, where the audience are guests at the absurdly pretentious wedding of the daughter of the former Prime Minister, José María Aznar… These plays, like the rest of his output, are endlessly imaginative, boldly conceived pieces of theatre whose shifting paradigms of performance take an audience into the very heart of their action, but that also unsettle and force new perspectives.

NOCTURNAL

Within this context, *Nocturnal* (*Animales nocturnos*) can be seen as a work of geometric precision. The circularity of the story line takes us into the heart of a sense that oppression is always with us, no matter how much we convince ourselves that it is the product of exceptional circumstances – a dramatic evocation of Foucault's panopticon, as Gwynneth Dowling notes in her study of the state of exception in Mayorga's theatre. But this circle of watchfulness sits on top of a number of intersecting parallels, creating in their own way other echoes of inevitability and enclosure. It may well be that love and friendship are ways out of, or through, these strict geometries, but the play also suggests the imbalances, the asymmetries, and the self-deceptions that dog our every attempt to break away.

The play started out as a one act piece – *The Good Neighbour (El buen vecino)* – and like so many of this writer's plays has continued as a work in progress, undergoing most recently a series of re-writes for this English-language premiere at the Gate. This apparent sense of dissatisfaction with his own work, a key element of Juan Mayorga's artistic sensibility, is clearly not reflected in the wave of prizes – including the prestigious Spanish National Theatre Prize –and acclaimed international productions that his theatre has attracted and inspired. It is certainly an indication of his willingness to work collaboratively with new directors, actors and translators, to re-assess as new sensibilities engage with his plays. But more importantly it is a statement of ethics, an affirmation that theatre, at its most effective, its most far-reaching, is of necessity provisional and framed by the moment in which it is performed. This is a theatre that continually experiments with form, that constantly unsettles and displaces the audience. Of course such displacement is a way of counteracting the certainties of belonging, of ownership, of supremacy of being that are the major sources of discrimination and conflict in the biopolitics of our time. This is where Juan Mayorga's work is acutely political in its effect and vision, but draws upon, and enriches itself from, the radical philosophical tradition of Montaigne, Kant, Benjamin and Agamben.

OUT OF THE WINGS

Out of the Wings is an AHRC-funded project whose purpose is to make plays written in Spanish available to English-language theatre practitioners. Inevitably, Juan Mayorga's theatre features there, and will continue to feature, strongly. For further information, go to www.outofthewings.org.uk

David Johnston
Belfast, April 2009

Characters

SHORT MAN

TALL MAN

TALL WOMAN

SHORT WOMAN

Voices:
DOCTOR, OLD MAN, OLD WOMAN,
AQUARIUS, PISCES, ARIES

1

SHORT MAN:	Do you mind if I sit down?
TALL MAN:	I was just about to get the bill.
SHORT MAN:	Do you not recognise me? You don't know who I am?
TALL MAN:	?
SHORT MAN:	We see each other every day.
TALL MAN:	?
SHORT MAN:	Every morning. On the stairs. I'm going out just as you get in.
TALL MAN:	Of course.
SHORT MAN:	'*Morn*ing'. Ring a bell?
TALL MAN:	It does now, yes.
SHORT MAN:	Though it sounds different at this time of the day, on a Sunday afternoon, than it does at six o'clock on a weekday morning.
TALL MAN:	I'm sorry… I didn't recognise you.
SHORT MAN:	No need to be sorry. Perfectly fine. If you don't mind, I will sit down. Perfectly fine. You get home, a shadow, and you pass another shadow on the stairs. '*Morn*ing' you hear, and you say '*Morn*ing' back. That's all there is to it. Two shadows passing on the stairs.
TALL MAN:	No, you're right.
SHORT MAN:	It can't be easy. Working nights, I mean. Your whole life's back to front.

TALL MAN: You'll have to excuse me, I was in a hurry.

SHORT MAN: I've just ordered this bottle. And two glasses. I'd like us to have a drink together.

TALL MAN: I'm sorry, I don't drink.

SHORT MAN: It's just that I'm celebrating… I thought you might like to keep me company.

TALL MAN: I'm expected.

SHORT MAN: Go on, just one.

TALL MAN: I told you… I don't drink.

SHORT MAN: Just a few moments of your time. It's not much fun celebrating on your own.

TALL MAN: All right. A few moments. Seeing as you're celebrating.

SHORT MAN: 1998. I'm no connoisseur. But I wanted to get it right. I did some research.

TALL MAN: Good news, then, eh? Something to celebrate. Lucky man.

SHORT MAN: Isn't this great? Two shadows pass each other on the stairs every morning and for months on end the only thing they say is '*Morn*ing' '*Morn*ing'. And now here we are, sitting at the same table, celebrating together.

TALL MAN: Months? Have we known each other for months?

SHORT MAN: I didn't mean anything by it. You've always been polite, always ready to say hello. You couldn't say that of all our neighbours. But until today, that's what we were, two strangers who said good morning as they went about their business. And now look at us, sitting here, celebrating, as if we had known each other all our lives.

TALL MAN: You still haven't told me what we're celebrating.

SHORT MAN: Have I not? All this talking and I still haven't told you…?

TALL MAN: Not yet.

SHORT MAN: It's just that it's strange being here with you, I mean here. Do you know what I mean? Every Sunday, after finishing in the kitchen, I go out for a walk. And I see you in here, at this table. I mean from the outside, through the glass. I must have seen you a hundred times sitting at this table. Didn't you ever notice me?

TALL MAN: Sorry.

SHORT MAN: No, I don't mean anything by it. I'm used to not being noticed. I'm not the sort to push himself forward. You've probably never heard any of the neighbours even mention me. I'm not the sort of neighbour who gets talked about. Mind you, I pride myself on being a good neighbour. Anyone who knocks on my door knows I'll always…

TALL MAN: I don't want to leave without knowing what we're celebrating.

SHORT MAN: Section 3754.

TALL MAN: Sorry…

SHORT MAN: You don't know what it is?

TALL MAN:	Section 3574, you said?
SHORT MAN:	3754. More commonly called the Immigration Act. That's what people call it.
TALL MAN:	I didn't realise you were…
SHORT MAN:	I'm not. I'm not a foreigner.
TALL MAN:	In that case?
SHORT MAN:	But you are. A foreigner.
TALL MAN:	Me?
SHORT MAN:	I may know very little about you. But I do know that. The basics.
TALL MAN:	Look, you really will have to excuse me. It's getting late.
SHORT MAN:	Please sit where you are. Please, sit down. Thank you. Listen, I've nothing against foreigners. Nothing at all, no matter where they're from. I don't know what it was brought you to this country. Work? Politics? A woman? Whatever it was, I don't care. And I didn't make the law. But as soon as I heard about it, I knew it was going to change my life. Well, not straight away I didn't. But I thought about it and it was only today I decided to put my idea into practice. Listen, I'm serious, I've nothing against any of you. It's nothing personal. I just thought I should concentrate on one case, and yours is the one I know best.
TALL MAN:	I'm not sure if I understand, I don't think I do. But let's be clear on one thing: I'm not foreign.

SHORT MAN:	You're not?
TALL MAN:	Of course I'm not. What made you think I am? Just because I work nights? So do a lot of people.
SHORT MAN:	You're not foreign?
TALL MAN:	No. Do I look foreign?
SHORT MAN:	No.
TALL MAN:	I've nothing against them, as long as they don't bring their problems to our door. I've known people of every hue and shade, good people. People who don't come and tell you how to live in your own country. Unfortunately, there seems to be more and more of the other sort, who…
SHORT MAN:	There's no need; that's more than enough. I've got to hand it to you. Congratulations. You're accent is better than mine, and the way you use the language…the way you gesture, the way you move… Remarkable discipline. I admire people with self-control. Don't worry, it's not that you've done anything wrong, I never suspected anything, it was just a hunch. I made some enquiries, anyone can, you just need to put a little bit of time into it. And I came up trumps. My hunch was right. You've no papers. You're an illegal immigrant.
TALL MAN:	That's not true.
SHORT MAN:	Then show them to me. Your papers.
TALL MAN:	Show them to you? Who do you think you are? I've had enough of this.

SHORT MAN: What are you going to do? Start a row
               in front of everyone? Call the police?
               Go ahead. Relax. I haven't tried to insult
               you. All I said was that you're a foreigner,
               an illegal immigrant. No big deal, except
               that under Section 3754, you could be
               sent back home at once. Maybe it is
               3475?

TALL MAN: Have you been drinking?

SHORT MAN: Not a drop. I don't like drinking on my
               own. Please don't stand up again without
               me telling you to, don't make me do
               anything I don't want to. I'm trying to be
               friendly. I told you, it's nothing personal.
               I don't make the law. But it has changed
               our relationship. Two shadows that pass
               on the stairs every morning until one
               day…

TALL MAN: This is a joke.

SHORT MAN: I'm not very good with jokes. No, it's not
               a joke. To put it crudely…well, if I were a
               crude sort of person, I could say, 'I've got
               you by the balls'.

TALL MAN: You *are* drunk.

SHORT MAN: There's no need for that. Am I not being
               respectful with you? I could insult you. I
               could have you on your knees…

TALL MAN: What is it you want? Once and for all.
               Money?

SHORT MAN: Money?

TALL MAN: What is it you want?

SHORT MAN: Nothing much.

TALL MAN: What?

SHORT MAN: I don't know yet. Honestly, I don't. For
the time being, I just want you to have
a drink with me. That'll do for today.
Tomorrow, who knows? I'll think of
something. But it'll never be anything…
dubious, I can promise you that. Nothing
to do with sex, ever. You're lucky it's
me. I'm not going to make you work for
me or commit a crime or lay a finger
on you. One day, I might ask for a bit
of conversation, the next to go for a
walk with me. Nothing terrible, nothing
degrading. Get you to read me a poem,
or tell me a joke… Nothing degrading.
Occasionally I'll ask you to do something
uncomfortable, or unpleasant, not to
offend you, just to make sure you're
willing. That's what it's about, what
matters: making sure you're willing.
Some days I'll let you forget all about
me, but I'll always come back. And I'll
ask you to recite something or sing a
song from where you're from, not to
be offensive, just to remind you of our
relationship. Never to degrade you. And
maybe one day you'll be made legal. In
the meantime, let's get on with our lives.
Tomorrow, at the usual time, we'll cross
on the stairs and say good morning. I
want you to be there. Don't try and run
away. I'm going to be watching. And
don't ever think of trying anything. I've
already thought about that. I'm a man
who thinks ahead. I won't ask you to do
anything degrading, you can count on
that. We'll start straight away. We'll begin
by sharing this bottle. Perhaps I could

make a toast. For you. For a new life, in
the old country.

Pause. The TALL MAN drinks.

2

*The TALL WOMAN is working at a table covered in papers. She doesn't
notice the TALL MAN has come home. He surprises her with a kiss.*

TALL MAN:	What went wrong? I was waiting for you.
TALL WOMAN:	How did it go? Okay?
TALL MAN:	Are you all right? I thought we were going to…
TALL WOMAN:	I *was* there. I went to look for you.
TALL MAN:	I was there all afternoon.
TALL WOMAN:	I didn't go in. I saw you from outside.
TALL MAN:	?
TALL WOMAN:	You were with our upstairs neighbour.
TALL MAN:	Why didn't you come in?
TALL WOMAN:	I didn't want to interrupt.
TALL MAN:	You didn't want to interrupt? Interrupt what?
TALL WOMAN:	You seemed to be enjoying yourselves. Do you know what time it is? I'll cook you something quick. What would you like?
TALL MAN:	Don't worry about that…sit down.
TALL WOMAN:	Something easy. An omelette.

TALL MAN:	I'll pick up a sandwich on the way to work. So we can talk for ten minutes. I want to tell you something.
TALL WOMAN:	Tell me.
TALL MAN:	We were supposed to have been going for a walk. It was a lovely day for a walk.
TALL WOMAN:	You seemed to be drinking to something.
TALL MAN:	Raining all week. But on Sunday, the sun comes out, a big yellow sun, like in a story. A perfect day for a walk.
TALL WOMAN:	It looked like wine. Was it? Wine?
TALL MAN:	He insisted on buying me a drink.
TALL WOMAN:	I thought: at last. A friend at last.
TALL MAN:	He's not my friend. He was celebrating, and he didn't want to do it on his own.
TALL WOMAN:	Well, that's good...isn't it? That there are still people capable of sharing their own happiness with others.
TALL MAN:	He was a pain.
TALL WOMAN:	Don't be like that.
TALL MAN:	A pain. (*He hears noises coming from the flat above.*) I was hoping you'd show up, to give me an excuse to leave. 'You must forgive me, dear neighbour. Very interesting conversation, but my wife and I have arranged to take a stroll together.' He was a bore. He ruined my afternoon. With your connivance. Between the two of you, you spoiled my day.
TALL WOMAN:	What was he celebrating?
TALL MAN:	You wouldn't believe it if I told you.

TALL WOMAN:	He seems a nice sort. Not like his wife. Stuck up. Never says hello.
TALL MAN:	He's married then?
	The lights flicker.
TALL WOMAN:	That's the third time it's done that. The last time it went off for a while. There must be a loose wire.
TALL MAN:	We'll have to take a look. So he's married.
TALL WOMAN:	I've seen him with a woman.
TALL MAN:	I never imagined him married.
TALL WOMAN:	You must have seen her. In the park. (*She points out through the window.*) She usually sits over there, on the bench. Every morning, over there, feeding the pigeons.
TALL MAN:	Hard to imagine what sort of woman could be with a man like that.
TALL WOMAN:	Like that? Like what?
TALL MAN:	Such a pain.
TALL WOMAN:	You're too critical. Give him a chance. Not everyone can be brilliant. Is that what you wanted to tell me about him, that he's a bore?
TALL MAN:	I didn't see him, I didn't notice him there. He asked me if he could sit down. Very politely, very respectfully. He said he wanted to buy me a drink, that he was celebrating. How could I say no? And then he said… You wouldn't believe what he said. It's not even worth talking about.
TALL WOMAN:	What was it?

TALL MAN:	Nothing. Something stupid. So tell me… what have you been doing? (*He points at a package of books sitting on the table.*) The new consignment? Anything good? (*Looking at the books in the package.*) Safety first for submariners, a catalogue of electrical appliances…and three new Arizona Kid novels! 'Ten Bullets of Gold', 'City Outside the Law', 'Ghost Train'!
TALL WOMAN:	And a book of poems.
TALL MAN:	Any good?
TALL WOMAN:	Terrible. But there's a good quotation at the beginning.
	The TALL MAN finds the book and the quotation, He reads.
TALL MAN:	'The fox knows many things. The hedgehog, only one. But what he knows is important.' (*Trying to remember.*) Aesop?
TALL WOMAN:	Archilocus. So this neighbour, he said something stupid.
TALL MAN:	What do you know about him? Where does he work?
TALL WOMAN:	No idea. Did he say something to annoy you?
TALL MAN:	It's what you said. Not everyone can be brilliant.
TALL WOMAN:	But what did he say?
TALL MAN:	He was all right until he started on literature. If you'd heard the sort of stuff he likes. There I was having to listen to his nonsense instead of talking a walk with my wife.

TALL WOMAN:	It can't have been that bad. If it'd been as awful as you say, you'd have got up and left. You don't suffer fools gladly.
TALL MAN:	I felt sorry for him. Every time I tried to get up, he looked at me like an abandoned puppy. Anyway, what about you? You didn't come in because you thought I was with my new best friend. So what did you do? Let me guess…you came back home to the Arizona Kid.
TALL WOMAN:	Actually, I didn't. It would have been such a shame to stay indoors. A big yellow sun, like in a story. So I went for a walk. I just walked.
TALL MAN:	Just walked?
TALL WOMAN:	I suddenly noticed men were looking at me.
TALL MAN:	Looking at you? Men were?
TALL WOMAN:	They turned their heads.
TALL MAN:	Men were looking at you? Why? Were you wearing that purple jumper again?
TALL WOMAN:	No. I looked really lovely.
TALL MAN:	Really lovely, you? No.
TALL WOMAN:	They thought I did. There was one man especially, with a hat.
TALL MAN:	A man with a hat. In that sun? Was he bald?
TALL WOMAN:	I noticed him following me… I could hear his footsteps behind me. And then it struck me. What if he's just going the same way as me? Maybe he doesn't like me at all. Perhaps I've just imagined it.

TALL MAN: Perhaps.

TALL WOMAN: But I wasn't just imagining it. I sat down on a bench and he sat down beside me.

TALL MAN: He sat down beside you? No wonder I felt like I'd been abandoned. No wonder I've been feeling abandoned all afternoon.

TALL WOMAN: Are his tastes so bad…our neighbour? Let me try and guess what sort of books he reads. Thrillers? Love stories? He looks like somebody who'd like love stories.

TALL MAN: Love? If only you knew what he was celebrating. Anyway, do we know any electricians?

TALL WOMAN: I don't. What was he celebrating?

TALL MAN: Don't change the subject. So the man with the hat sat down beside you. I'm not sure I like that, but I forgive you.

TALL WOMAN: He sat down beside me and he spoke to me.

TALL MAN: He spoke to you! Did he?

TALL WOMAN: Have you got your bag ready?

TALL MAN: He sat down beside you and spoke to you.

TALL WOMAN: 'Lovely day, isn't it. The sort of sun you get in storybooks, don't you think so? I don't know your name, Miss…?'

TALL MAN: So was he bald or not?

TALL WOMAN: That's him over there. (*Pointing out through the window.*) Standing over by the fountain. No, you can't see him now. He's hiding behind the trees.

TALL MAN: I scared him off. He saw me and took fright. That's the last we'll see of him. You'll have to make do with me.

He hugs her.

TALL WOMAN: What are you doing? You're going to be late. Your bag. Make sure you've got everything. Your notebook, your sandwich, fruit, water. Or would you rather have wine? Now you've got a taste for it… Your hands are cold.

The lights flicker. Noise from the flat above.

3

SHORT WOMAN: I was worried.

SHORT MAN: You're right, I should have called you. It went clean out of my mind. What's that smell? You've been cooking?

SHORT WOMAN: It didn't turn out.

SHORT MAN: Why didn't you look in the fridge? There was meat from yesterday.

SHORT WOMAN: I remembered that stew, with the mushrooms, the one you liked. I think I overcooked it. I was about to throw it out.

The SHORT MAN tastes the stew.

SHORT MAN: It's okay. It is overcooked, but it doesn't taste bad. (*Savouring.*) Maybe the vinegar though… It's always hard to judge the

	vinegar. I'm not hungry anyway. Have you been in all afternoon?
SHORT WOMAN:	In case you phoned.
SHORT MAN:	All afternoon, watching the TV?
SHORT WOMAN:	A bit. Not really. I was cooking.
SHORT MAN:	I don't know how you do it. The TV gets worse every day. Everything's shit nowadays. What about the novel I gave you? Have you finished it?
SHORT WOMAN:	Yes. Not yet. I'm halfway through. I remembered that stew. Do you remember that little village, the first time we went on holiday? That restaurant you found. What was the name of that little village?
SHORT MAN:	I don't remember.

He takes out his tool box.

SHORT WOMAN:	Will I defrost the meat?
SHORT MAN:	You have it. I'm not hungry.

Silence. The MAN begins repairing a lamp. As he works, he makes the noises that were heard in the flat below.

SHORT WOMAN:	I thought: he'll be cleaning the car.
SHORT MAN:	I should have called.
SHORT WOMAN:	Then I thought: he'll have gone to watch the trains.
SHORT MAN:	Have you been at this?
SHORT WOMAN:	No.
SHORT MAN:	You didn't take the small screwdriver?

SHORT WOMAN:	No, I don't think so. Why didn't you wake me up?
SHORT MAN:	I didn't want to. You needed to sleep. You were worn out this morning.
SHORT WOMAN:	I must have slept for ages. Four hours, maybe more.
SHORT MAN:	What time did you stay up to, watching the telly last night? I heard you getting up.
SHORT WOMAN:	I couldn't sleep. With the trains.
SHORT MAN:	You can't hear them. They're too far away.
SHORT WOMAN:	The fish make me nervous. Just being there, floating around, while we're sleeping.
SHORT MAN:	What's on at that time? Films?
SHORT WOMAN:	It's better than daytime. Are you nearly finished?
SHORT MAN:	I popped into the Jakarta for a drink. I bumped into our downstairs neighbour.
SHORT WOMAN:	I don't know why you do so much.
SHORT MAN:	If I don't, who will?
SHORT WOMAN:	You don't get any thanks for it.
SHORT MAN:	What matters is that things get done. Have you seen the state the front door downstairs is in? It's a disgrace. A coat of paint and this lamp will look like new.
SHORT WOMAN:	But it's not just things for the residents' association. You fix children's toys, a broken cistern for some woman, a radio for somebody else. You can't say no.

34

You've never a minute to yourself. People take advantage.

SHORT MAN: Well, we know what people are like. They know I can turn my hand to most things. Do you know what my secret is? Care. I take care with things.

SHORT WOMAN: If you tell me what you're doing, maybe I can help you.

SHORT MAN: Don't worry, I've almost finished.

SHORT WOMAN: Do you mind if I watch you?

SHORT MAN: Of course not.

Silence.

SHORT WOMAN: I've been trying to remember all afternoon. That little village, there was a square, with a band in it.

SHORT MAN: This is the tricky bit.

SHORT WOMAN: We went there a few times, we danced…

SHORT MAN: It's tighter than I thought.

SHORT WOMAN: You asked how they did it and the owner wrote it out on a paper napkin. And you made it when we got home, and it was perfect. We used to have it every Sunday.

SHORT MAN: It's stew. That's all.

Silence. The WOMAN sits down to eat the stew.

SHORT WOMAN: There's a programme for people who can't sleep. It starts at midnight. People phone in to talk about themselves, how long they haven't been able to sleep for, the problems they have. Like at work. There's a doctor who asks you questions and then tells you what you can do. 'Go

35

and live in the country.' Or 'Change your job'. Apparently there's more and more people suffering from sleeplessness.

SHORT MAN: It's not insomnia you've got. It's just a word. But you'll end up having it if you keep on sitting up to watch TV. Are you sure you've not been at the small screwdriver?

SHORT WOMAN: I don't think so. Why would I?

SHORT MAN: You must have been.

Silence.

It's the most ridiculous thing I've ever heard. A late-night programme to cure insomnia. I bet that doctor doesn't give a toss about curing anyone.

SHORT WOMAN: Some people phone in to thank him. They've been cured.

SHORT MAN: He's a fraud. Those sort of programmes, they're all cons. I bet that doctor's selling something. Isn't he? Sleeping tablets or sleepy music.

SHORT WOMAN: He's not selling anything.

SHORT MAN: Then the number you call in on. Premium rate? That's how they do their business. Fools and their money.

Silence.

What a world. If you're not an idiot, you're a crook.

Silence.

You must know who I mean. The tall man. You must have bumped into him on the stairs.

SHORT WOMAN: I know who you mean: the tall man.

SHORT MAN: You don't see much of her, do you? Have you ever spoken to her?

SHORT WOMAN: No, but she seems quite nice.

Silence. The SHORT WOMAN finishes eating. She looks through the window.

I don't know why they switch the fountain off at night. It can't cost that much.

The MAN looks at her. When she returns his gaze, he looks down at the lamp again. Silence.

Your birthday…is there anything you'd like?

SHORT MAN: It's a month away.

SHORT WOMAN: I never seem to get it right.

SHORT MAN: Why do you think that? You've very good taste.

SHORT WOMAN: Look at last year… I can't even remember what I got you.

Silence.

SHORT MAN: The green shirt. It was a lovely present.

SHORT WOMAN: The green shirt? I don't remember it.

Silence.

Why don't you stop now?

SHORT MAN: I don't like leaving things half done, you know that.

Silence. She kisses him goodnight.

Those programmes are for idiots. You're not an idiot. Ordinary people spend their whole lives sitting in front of the TV, but you're not an ordinary person. If you're going to bed, would you mind feeding the fish on your way? No, don't bother, I'll do it.

Silence. The WOMAN goes towards the bedroom, but stops.

SHORT WOMAN: I must have taken it…to tighten something. I must have just set it down somewhere.

She goes out. He continues working in silence.

SHORT MAN: Gotcha, my friend.

The lamp switches on. The SHORT MAN smiles.

4

The SHORT MAN and the TALL MAN are seated facing the audience. Occasionally their eyes move as though following the movement of something. Long silence.

SHORT MAN: They look harmless, don't they? But in the dark they can be dangerous.

Silence.

I wonder what they make of us. Just imagine how you would feel if people sat down to watch what you're doing. How would you feel? I'm asking you.

TALL MAN: There aren't that many people who do watch them.

SHORT MAN: No, you're right. Not that many people are interested in them. Very few people come in here and almost nobody stops to look. How long have we been here?

TALL MAN: Half an hour?

SHORT MAN: And nobody's sat down to watch. Just us. The notice outside puts people off. 'Nocturnals'. I don't know what they imagine might be in here, but most people don't come in. And the few that do, you can see they don't like the dark.

TALL MAN: No.

SHORT MAN: This must be special glass, do you not think? They look sort of shiny. It must be special glass, special lighting too, so that you can see them in the dark without them being disturbed. But it's true: people come in and then go out again, as if they'd seen something terrible. Did you hear what that old man said to the boy? 'It's creepy.' Do you think it is...creepy?

TALL MAN: Well, it's not my favourite place in the zoo. I like the outside.

SHORT MAN: But you must admit it's well done, isn't it? It's hard to tell what's real and what's not. The rocks, the trees, the sky, the moon. Do you think these creatures know that none of it's real?

TALL MAN: I don't know.

SHORT MAN: That water? Do you think they can really drink it?

TALL MAN: I don't know.

SHORT MAN:	I wonder what life's like in here when the zoo's closed. When it's night-time outside. Do they switch on a light for them, like an artificial sun? So that they can sleep. Do they make them believe it's daytime?
TALL MAN:	I don't know.
SHORT MAN:	Sit down again. I want you to look at them from here.

Pause. The TALL MAN sits down again.

I'm making a night train. Whenever I have the time. Not an ordinary one, you know, with a couple of little lights. I'm talking about a moon and electric stars. And the atmosphere, specially…you have to see it on the little figures. The other night, at the station, did you notice the people? People who travel at night are different. One of these days you'll have to come to upstairs to have a look and you'll see what I mean. Are you tired?

TALL MAN:	No.
SHORT MAN:	Am I boring you?
TALL MAN:	I don't know much about animals.
SHORT MAN:	Have you never had any?
TALL MAN:	No.
SHORT MAN:	I used to have a dog, when I was small. Not now though. You can't keep the place clean when there's an animal.
TALL MAN:	What's that one?
SHORT MAN:	A skunk. People mix it up with the badger. Does it not put you in mind of

the twins on the third floor? With their airs and graces, and all show.

TALL MAN: (*Pointing.*) That's a... I didn't know that hedgehogs...

SHORT MAN: There are more nocturnals than you would think.

TALL MAN: A strange creature. A strange creature even among strange creatures. 'The fox knows many things. The hedgehog, only one. But what he knows is important.'

SHORT MAN: ?

TALL MAN: A story from the 'Arabian Nights'. That's how it starts: 'The fox knows many things. The hedgehog, only one. But what he knows is important.'

Silence.

SHORT MAN: You can see how well-read you are. In the café, the park, I used to see you all the time, with a book in your hand. Good books, not rubbish. And writing things down in your little notebook. I could tell. What about me? Am I like what you imagined? I'm not so bad, am I? Is there anything I can do for you? What about work? You hear terrible things about... discrimination.

TALL MAN: I've been lucky.

SHORT MAN: And the flat?

TALL MAN: It's okay. The light goes every now and then, but it's comfortable enough.

SHORT MAN: I bumped into your wife again yesterday. The way she looks at me...she doesn't like me, but she doesn't know why she doesn't like me. You haven't told her, have you?

Silence.

What have you told her?

Silence.

In that case we have a secret, you and me. A secret.

Silence.

TALL MAN: That owl's huge.

SHORT MAN: It's not an ordinary owl. It's a barn owl. It's as if he was looking at us. Do you think he is?

TALL MAN: Could be.

SHORT MAN: Look at me. I move and he follows me with his eyes. I walk and he follows me. He's watching us. What do you think he makes of us, you and me?

TALL MAN: Who knows?

SHORT MAN: He'll be wondering…he's seen me so many times on my own. And suddenly, here I am, with you.

TALL MAN: Is that your favourite, the barn owl?

SHORT MAN: He doesn't miss a thing. That's a real virtue. But there are creatures I like more.

TALL MAN: What do you think about that one, on the rock, with the red fur?

SHORT MAN: He loves being the centre of attention. I've got colleagues like that. (*To the animal.*) You'll learn soon enough: people that don't do anything else other than show off, they're the losers.

TALL MAN: And that other one, over there?

SHORT MAN: It reminds me…

TALL MAN: Of?

SHORT MAN: He doesn't know where he's going… always scuttling about, but not knowing where he's going. He's like my wife.

Silence.

I've been lucky with her. She sees things in me that other people don't, and I can be sure of her, absolutely sure. She has her limitations, of course she does. Like the rest of us. Anyway, I'm partly to blame. But I've been the making of her too…sex as well… She hasn't been sleeping well lately. I can't imagine what that must be like, because I do. I've heard people saying it's like torture: not sleeping.

TALL MAN: Some people don't sleep because they're frightened of sleeping. A lot of things happen when you sleep.

SHORT MAN: A lot of things happen when you sleep? Is that another story? It sounds like the start of a story.

TALL MAN: No.

Silence.

SHORT MAN: It's a gift to have a way with words. Have you read 'The Diary of Anne Frank'? Of course you have. It's a famous book. I'm fascinated by that…that ability. I've tried several times…to keep a diary. But I've never managed it. It seemed ordinary. I couldn't express what I was living, which wasn't ordinary.

Silence.

You're like that one there.

TALL MAN: That one? Am I?

SHORT MAN: Walk over towards the door.

Pause. The TALL MAN walks. The SHORT MAN watches him.

Do you think it affects you, working at night? Physically.

TALL MAN: I don't think so.

SHORT MAN: And with your wife?

Silence.

She must be very special. Look, we won't talk about her if you don't want to. I'm not interested in her. It was you I chose. (*Looking again at the creature that resembles the TALL MAN.*) He's different from the rest. He walks like he was stepping on marble. But he's the most vulnerable of all. He needs protection. Look at that other one. Nobody pays him any attention. But he sees everything, things that might be useful one day. And he's patient. Patience is the greatest virtue of all.

TALL MAN: So he's your favourite?

SHORT MAN: We should be going. I don't want you to be late for work. We'll come back. I know people don't like this place. I'm

not surprised, I know what they're like.
They'll end up closing this place. Do
you know why people don't like them?
Because they're different, because they
live back to front. They're not likeable
creatures, children don't like them,
they have an aura. One day these poor
animals will get some sort of injection,
and they'll bring in sunnier creatures,
more colourful. That's what people like.
That's the way people are. I want you
to tell me that story tomorrow. The one
about the hedgehog and the fox.

5

*Moonless night. In the flat below the TALL MAN and the TALL WOMAN.
In the flat above, the SHORT MAN and the SHORT WOMAN. The SHORT
MAN gets out of bed and goes to where the SHORT WOMAN is watching
the television. The sound of adverts.*

SHORT MAN: Do you not think it's too loud?

SHORT WOMAN: What?

                 The SHORT MAN turns the sound down.

SHORT MAN: The neighbours will complain.

                 *The TALL MAN gets out of bed and goes to where
                 the TALL WOMAN is working.*

TALL MAN: I'm off one night in ten. And you're going
                 to spend it with the Arizona Kid?

TALL WOMAN: I'd have finished by now if they their TV
                 wasn't on so loud. I've a good mind to
                 say something.

TALL MAN:	You're trying to do too much, do you not think? You don't have to take so much on. We could get by with less.
TALL WOMAN:	We could get a smaller flat. Or we can try and save and move to a better area. How would you translate this?
TALL MAN:	If I translate it, will you come to bed?
TALL WOMAN:	From here.
TALL MAN:	(*Translating on sight.*) 'The muscles on his face contracted as he saw under the moonlight the unmistakeable trace of smoke... A few seconds later the ghost train was crossing...cutting through the valley. In one of those seemingly empty wagons, armed to the teeth, was...'

The light flickers and goes out.

TALL WOMAN:	Again.
SHORT MAN:	They're even more mindless than during the day. You've only got to look at those adverts to imagine the sort of people goggling at them. Even the thought of it.
SHORT WOMAN:	The programme's got nothing to do with the adverts. It's an interesting case tonight. A married couple. They both became insomniacs at the same time. They blame each other.
TALL WOMAN:	You said you were going to get somebody who understands electrics.
SHORT WOMAN:	The doctor has worked out they don't trust each other.

The light comes back on in the flat above.

	It was her called in. But you can tell he's OK. When he was small, he didn't feel loved.
TALL MAN:	(*Returning to the translation.*) 'In one of those seemingly empty wagons, armed to the teeth, was his greatest enemy.'
TALL WOMAN:	That's the problem. He's not just his enemy. He's his best friend too. That's clear from the original. You can't just translate it as 'enemy'.
TALL MAN:	'…armed to the teeth, was his greatest…' Say anything. How much are they paying you per page? Who reads Arizona Kid novels anyway? Half a dozen nutcases on the bus. Put whatever you want and come to bed.
TALL WOMAN:	I can't put anything. Especially not here. This is the climax of the novel.
TALL MAN:	Of course you can. (*He lifts a pen and paper and makes the following up, ignoring the original.*) 'In one of those seemingly empty wagons, armed to the teeth, was the only man who had ever been his match. Without a backward glance, Arizona galloped down the hill…' (*He continues writing in silence.*)
SHORT WOMAN:	You forgot to feed the fish this Sunday.
SHORT MAN:	Did I?
SHORT WOMAN:	Are you thinking about something?
SHORT MAN:	Everything's fine. Why don't you go to bed? Even if you don't sleep, you'll still rest.
SHORT WOMAN:	I'll turn it off in a minute.

SHORT MAN: Did you go out last night? I thought I heard the door.

SHORT WOMAN: I went for a walk.

SHORT MAN: At that time?

SHORT WOMAN: I was fed up tossing and turning in bed.

SHORT MAN: You know I've never been one for pills, but sometimes there's no choice. We'll go and get you a prescription tomorrow.

SHORT WOMAN: Have you thought about what you want for your birthday yet?

SHORT MAN: Anything. I'm going to make the Sunday lunch tomorrow. I'll be out all day Sunday.

TALL MAN: (*Finishing writing.*) Oh, I forgot to tell you. The day after tomorrow. The neighbour upstairs has asked me to do something for him.

TALL WOMAN: On Sunday?

TALL MAN: He's going to visit his father. He lives out of town. He's asked me to go with him. I don't think they get on too well. He probably thinks that if there's someone else there, it'll help smooth things over. The truth is I couldn't say no. Again.

SHORT MAN: It's been a long time since I went to see my father. I'm not going to ask you to come with me this time. I know you're polite with him, but there's always something that irritates him. Maybe you could go and see your sister's children. When was the last time you saw them?

TALL WOMAN:	It's not a problem. I was planning on going out on Sunday as well.
TALL MAN:	You were?
TALL WOMAN:	The man with the hat. I don't know how he got my number. I swear I didn't give it to him. I don't know what to make of him. At first I thought he was a fox. But he's persistent. Like a hedgehog.
TALL MAN:	?
TALL WOMAN:	'The fox knows many things. The hedgehog, only one. But what he knows is important.' Do you think he was just talking about animals?
TALL MAN:	And what if he wasn't?
TALL WOMAN:	Maybe what he meant was that all human beings can be divided into two: hedgehogs and foxes. Generally speaking, I think I can tell the difference. Generally speaking, when I meet somebody, I know almost straight away if they're a hedgehog or a fox. But the man with the hat, well, I'm not sure.

Silence. The TALL MAN begins writing again, without looking at the original.

TALL MAN:	'It was all or nothing, a duel to the death. Two shots rang out.'

Change of channel on the television. The SHORT WOMAN turns up the volume. The TALL MAN and the TALL WOMAN look up at the flat above.

SHORT MAN:	Is that him? I never imagined him like that. With that hat.

SHORT WOMAN:	He wears a different hat every night.
SHORT MAN:	Some people have no sense of the ridiculous. I'm not going to ask you not to watch any more. Just allow the rest of us to get some sleep.
SHORT WOMAN:	I'm going to turn it off.

The SHORT MAN goes back to bed. The SHORT WOMAN shuts the door to the living room.

DOCTOR'S VOICE:	Friends, friends in the night, we're back with you again. Keeping you company through the night. The city is asleep, the whole country is asleep, but you and I, we're wide awake. Perhaps some secret is keeping us awake. Perhaps, without even being aware of it, you have some sort of mission, just like I have. Has that ever occurred to you, Aquarius? That you won't be able to sleep until you've carried out your mission?
AQUARIUS' VOICE:	My younger sister. I've got to help her. She's having an affair with a married man.
DOCTOR'S VOICE:	That's why you can't sleep. You're worn out, but you can't sleep. You have a mission.
TALL MAN:	'There he was, in front of him, bleeding, the man he feared and loved so much. But who was it who had fired, wondered Arizona. It wasn't him. He hadn't managed to draw, paralysed by fear. He heard a laugh behind him, as pure as crystal, and suddenly he understood everything. Dakota Kitty, the woman who when danger was at its height always

appeared on cue. The lovely gunslinger, more beautiful than ever.'

The TALL MAN takes the TALL WOMAN to bed. The SHORT WOMAN is listening to her mobile phone, waiting to go on.

DOCTOR'S VOICE: Gemini, hello. How are you tonight?

SHORT WOMAN: (*Into her phone.*) Better, much better.

DOCTOR'S VOICE: How have the nights been for you recently?

SHORT WOMAN: (*Into her phone.*) I think I'm getting there. Yesterday, I managed to sleep for three hours in one go. I did everything you told me to, I threw the shoes out and I moved the fish tank out of the bedroom... Him? He's in the bedroom, asleep... No, he won't be able to hear me... No, I haven't mentioned the dancing yet, I haven't had the chance... In the sitting room, I'm in the sitting room... On my own, apart from the fish. They're nocturnals, African fish... Yes, doctor, I will, I think so... No, I don't get anxious if I don't fall asleep right away... Do you think it would do me good to go back to work? It's just that I've been thinking... It's just that I'd need more time to explain everything... No, I understand, I know there are other people waiting. And they have things to say too... Thank you for talking to me, Doctor. Good night, Doctor.

Silence. The SHORT WOMAN puts away her phone. Pause. She stands up, but then sits down again.

6

Moonlit night. The TALL WOMAN has fallen asleep at her work. She is woken by the doorbell. Surprised, she looks at her watch. The bell rings again. She looks at the door, and walks over to it.

TALL WOMAN:	Who is it?
SHORT MAN:	Your neighbour. From upstairs.

The WOMAN hesitates.

Your husband told me about the electric going off. I was going to take a look at it. I understand electrics. Or would you rather I came back later?

Pause. The TALL WOMAN opens the door. The SHORT MAN comes in, carrying his tool box.

TALL WOMAN:	It's very kind of you. But there's no rush. It's not a big problem.
SHORT MAN:	Let's see. Where's the fuse-box?
TALL WOMAN:	There.

The SHORT MAN takes out his screwdrivers, chooses one and opens the fuse-box.

SHORT MAN:	How long's this been going on?
TALL WOMAN:	For the last month. All of a sudden, it began to flicker and then it just went out. But it comes back after a while. Can I get you a drink of anything?
SHORT MAN:	I'm fine, thanks.
TALL WOMAN:	Is there anything I can do?
SHORT MAN:	Don't worry, I can sort this one out.
TALL WOMAN:	I've heard you can fix anything. Watches, toys, trains…

SHORT MAN:	Did he tell you about the train?
TALL WOMAN:	He loved it. The lights, the little figures… can I hold that for you?
SHORT MAN:	Don't worry. You carry on with whatever you were doing. Lot of dictionaries.
TALL WOMAN:	There are, yes.
SHORT MAN:	Do you speak a lot of languages?
TALL WOMAN:	I get by.
SHORT MAN:	Have you lived in all those countries?
TALL WOMAN:	Some of them.
SHORT MAN:	Not like me. I've never been abroad.

She has returned to the table. He peers into the fuse-box. Silence.

It seems to be working. There may be a spot of damp touching the wire. Nothing to worry about, but it might be a good idea to take a proper look.

TALL WOMAN:	I haven't noticed any damp patches.
SHORT MAN:	You don't always see them. There's a switch here, so the wire must come down here. (*He runs his hands down the wall.*) There's probably a junction here. That is if they've done it with any sense. (*He comes to a photograph hanging on the wall.*) Beautiful children. (*Seeing another photograph.*) Lovely view. (*He continues to probe the walls in silence.*) That's the problem with these old buildings; split pipes, leaks… And if there are any wires nearby, well… You have to find out where it is, fix it, and close it up again. You can't mess around where there's

electricity; you can't trust it, just when you least expect it, it can turn on you.

Feeling the wall, he goes into the bedroom. The WOMAN stands up, but not in time to stop him. She watches him from the bedroom door. Silence. He emerges from the bedroom, still feeling the wall.

Beautiful bedspread. Lovely pattern, very colourful. Did you embroider it yourself?

TALL WOMAN: My mother.

SHORT MAN: Very soft to the touch. (*He rubs his fingers, like a caress. Until his gaze settles on a point on the wall.*) Gotcha, my friend, there you are; oh yes. Here it is, come over here. (*He takes the WOMAN's hand, and makes her touch the damp patch.*) Can you feel it? Can you feel the damp? Soft, like a body?

She pulls her hand away; she dries it. He selects a chisel from his collection of chisels; he puts out the light and switches on a torch, which he shines onto the damp patch on the wall.

Have to open the wall up here. There's no sign of anything from the outside, but once it's open you'll see soon enough. Cut out the bad.

But the WOMAN puts on the light.

TALL WOMAN: I'm very grateful. We'll take care of it. You must forgive me. I'm very busy.

The MAN puts his tools away.

SHORT MAN: Of course, this isn't the time. I hope I haven't said anything to upset you. I certainly didn't mean to. Your flat's very nice. Good taste. Good use of space.

He goes towards the door, from where he contemplates the house.

I didn't imagine it to be as small as this. The flats upstairs are much bigger. It's not fair. It's not right that a man like your husband should be living like this. A man of his abilities.

TALL WOMAN: We're fine here.

SHORT MAN: But it isn't right. A man of his quality.

TALL WOMAN: It's true, he does deserve better. But as Virgil said, a great man makes even the smallest place seem great. Have you read Virgil?

The SHORT MAN shakes his head. She points to a book on the shelves.

It is a small flat. But look at the library of books we have, the world's great books. The first thing we put into our cases: our books. And if we could only take one case, we'd fill that one with books. And even if the case was stolen… The important things are in here (*She touches her forehead.*) and in here. (*She puts her hand over her heart.*) You're getting to know my husband. There's one thing that nobody will ever be able to take from him. Just because you step into someone's shoes for a while, it doesn't give you what they have inside. One day we will have a bigger flat, or a house. For the time being, though, we've got everything we need. When two people have stuck together through thick and thin, it doesn't matter where they live. Anywhere's good as long as you stick together.

The SHORT MAN opens the door.

SHORT MAN: You're right. The important thing is to stick together.

He makes to leave and stops.

It's my birthday tomorrow. I won't have time. I'll be down the day after to finish this off.

He goes out. The WOMAN closes the door.

7

The TALL MAN's work place. There is a panel with numbers that light up, a blackboard and a small television. The MAN watches the Doctor's programme.

DOCTOR'S VOICE: Pisces, my friend, you're not alone The night is full of friends who want to get to know you.

PISCES' VOICE: I'm forty-eight years old and I've not slept for two years. I think I'm going mad.

DOCTOR'S VOICE: No. You have friends, lots of friends out there in the night, they won't let you go mad.

The TALL MAN is surprised by the arrival of the TALL WOMAN. Meanwhile, the television dialogue continues: 'PISCES – I feel very nervous... I've never spoken about this before. None of my family suspect. / DOCTOR – They don't know you're an insomniac? / PISCES – I pretend to be asleep.'

56

TALL MAN: What are you doing here? You shouldn't have come here.

TALL WOMAN: I've something to tell you.

TALL MAN: Could it not have waited? Do you want me to get the sack?

Silence. She is about to leave, but he stops her.

Sorry. You know how difficult it was to get this job. It's not your fault. Coffee?

The WOMAN sits down. He switches off the television and makes coffee. She looks around: objects to do with patient hygiene. She points at the panel.

TALL WOMAN: What's that?

TALL MAN: Room numbers. The old people have a button beside their beds. So we know if they need anything.

TALL WOMAN: Number five's lit.

TALL MAN: If he had his way, I'd spend the entire night up in his room. He'd talk all night.

TALL WOMAN: I didn't imagine it like this.

TALL MAN: I try and keep it as clean as I can, but the guy on the day shift leaves it in a terrible state. Can you smell it?

TALL WOMAN: Yes.

TALL MAN: He must spend the whole shift with a cigarette stuck in his mouth.

TALL WOMAN: Have you said anything? Did you say you don't like it?

TALL MAN: We hardly ever see each other. Anyway, it's not worth falling out over.

TALL WOMAN:	Is he from here?
TALL MAN:	He's from here, yes.

An OLD MAN is heard shouting: 'Noooo! Noooo!'
The TALL MAN doesn't seem to notice. He pours
the coffee.

TALL WOMAN:	The upstairs neighbour came down. Not long after you left.
TALL MAN:	Did he do anything to you? Did he say anything to you?
TALL WOMAN:	He was nosying round the whole flat. Pretending it was the lights. Did you ask him to fix them?
TALL MAN:	I don't remember saying anything. So he came down to help. It's a bit strange, but you can't say he's not willing. And he's good with his hands. Did he fix them? Did he find out what the problem is?
TALL WOMAN:	He says we have to cut into the wall. He said he'll do it. I don't want him in our house again.
TALL MAN:	Did he do anything unpleasant? No, I know he didn't pick the best moment to come. But apart from that?
TALL WOMAN:	Something about him. The way he was looking.
TALL MAN:	Always so worried. There's nothing to worry about. I'll go and thank him tomorrow and tell him we've found someone who'll take care of it for us. You shouldn't have let him in. You could have pretended to be asleep.

TALL WOMAN: I shouldn't have let him in? Why not? I thought he was your friend. You spend enough time with him.

TALL MAN: You can't always choose your friends. You can't always… (*Buzzer and number seventeen lights up. The TALL MAN presses a button and speaks into a microphone.*) Yes? What is it?

OLD MAN'S VOICE: I was caught short.

TALL MAN: I'll be up straight away. (*He lifts some clean sheets, and a bucket and mop.*) Nobody'll come, but if they do, tell them you're a relative of the lady in number six. And if the phone goes, just let it ring.

He goes out. The WOMAN looks around her. The OLD MAN shouts again: 'Noooo! Noooo!'. The phone rings. A buzzer and number fifteen lights up. The WOMAN switches on the television to drown out the sound.

DOCTOR'S VOICE: Life's a struggle, a battle, a war…that's what you were brought up believing. That's what they taught you…to be frightened for yourself and for the people you love. And now every night, Pisces, you're protecting the people you love. That's why you can't sleep. Because you're standing guard. Like a sentinel. But you're not on your own in the night, Pisces. Neither are you, Aries. We're out here, listening.

ARIES' VOICE: It's not myself I'm calling about. It's my son.

The telephone rings insistently. The WOMAN turns down the sound on the television and lifts the receiver. She listens to the voice on the other end. She hangs up as she hears the TALL MAN coming back. He comes in with his bucket and mop. And a cigarette that he shows the TALL WOMAN before throwing into the rubbish.

TALL MAN: He always gives me something. It's like a bribe. He's frightened that if he doesn't give me something, I won't go back. (*Pointing to the television.*) He looks like he knows what he's talking about. I suppose that's what they're all looking for when they call in. Like when you were small and you couldn't sleep, and you called for your daddy. (*He notices number fifteen is lit up, presses the button and speaks.*) Yes?

OLD WOMAN'S VOICE: My tablet.

TALL MAN: (*Looking at the blackboard.*) Not till four o'clock.

OLD WOMAN'S VOICE: My chest feels tight.

TALL MAN: I'm coming up. (*He takes a tablet and a glass of water. He points to the blackboard.*) Everything's written down here. At four o'clock take number fifteen her tablet; at half past four change number seven's bag… He thinks I'm his brother. I pretend I am. (*Pointing to the television.*) He's very good, the way he puts things into perspective. He makes them not feel guilty. (*He is about to go out.*)

TALL WOMAN: That man went into our bedroom. He touched our sheets.

Pause.

TALL MAN: He knows I'm illegal.

TALL WOMAN: Has he threatened you?

TALL MAN:	Do you remember that day you saw us in the café? He began talking to me about the law and…
TALL WOMAN:	So that's what it was. I didn't know what was going on. I should have gone in. I had the feeling something bad was going on, but I didn't dare, I left you on your own. It must have been awful. Why didn't you tell me?
TALL MAN:	I thought I could spare you this, now that things are going better for us. I thought it might just be some bad joke. Then when I realised he was serious…
TALL WOMAN:	Serious?
TALL MAN:	It still might be a bad joke.
TALL WOMAN:	Has he asked you…for anything? (*Buzzer and the light in fifteen blinks.*) Are you working for him?
TALL MAN:	He just wants…company, conversation.
TALL WOMAN:	We have to leave.
TALL MAN:	Not again. No.
TALL WOMAN:	What then?
TALL MAN:	I can deal with him.
TALL WOMAN:	Deal with him? How?
TALL MAN:	I've managed up to now. It hasn't been too bad so far.
TALL WOMAN:	Not too bad?
TALL MAN:	It's all so childish…you'd laugh if you saw us. Do you know what we were doing yesterday? Painting the figures for his train set. Little dolls!

TALL WOMAN: We'll go away. Tonight.

TALL MAN: We're going to let him drive us away? Now, when we're finally…

TALL WOMAN: Finally, what? A miserable flat and a shitty job. It doesn't smell of cigarettes. It smells of old men's piss.

TALL MAN: It has its good side. It's not always so busy. I can read. I can think.

TALL WOMAN: If we were still there, you'd be ashamed…

TALL MAN: Our life there is a different life. Forget it.

TALL WOMAN: Is there anything else? Anything you're not telling me about you and him?

TALL MAN: Anything else? Like what?

TALL WOMAN: Shall I tell you why I let him in? Because I wanted to know what he's like. (*Buzzer and light in fifteen.*) Now I know. I don't want you to see him again. We're going home and we're going to pack our bags.

TALL MAN: He won't let me go. He's thought it all through. There wouldn't even be any point in killing him. It has to be some other sort of solution, and I'm looking for it. Trust me. I know what I'm doing. Remember Sheherezade. Each time I'm with him, I try to think about Sheherezade. I'm taking it one day at a time. And if one day he loses interest in me, then we really are in danger. But if I become important to him, if I make him need me, then we're safe. We'll be more than safe. He's a poor fool. He almost comes if you quote Kafka at him. Give me a bit of time and I'll have him eating out of the palm of my hand.

TALL WOMAN: I'd rather he reported us. The telephone rang earlier. It was him. He'll call back. Tell him to go to the police.

TALL MAN: Why make him so important? He's not worth it. We've come through worse. You're always saying it: we're invincible as long as we keep our spirit intact.

TALL WOMAN: And our dignity?

TALL MAN: It's an unpleasant game, nothing else. One more unpleasant game.

TALL WOMAN: Do I know you? So many hardships, maybe they've confused us. We've looked after each other. Was it love? Maybe we've confused love with other things: solidarity, compassion…

TALL MAN: Give me time. He's changing, I'm changing him.

TALL WOMAN: Now I understand why his wife looks so defeated. Because she can't compete. No woman could, with a slave. Is that what you've chosen to be, his slave? I can't stand by and watch that happen. I'm getting on a train tomorrow, whether you come or not.

Silence.

TALL MAN: Half past four. (*He consults the blackboard.*) Number seven needs his sedative. He spent all last night shouting 'Turn that radio down you fucker. It's killing me!' He says the man next door keeps his radio full blast, just to annoy him. It's not true though. The man next door died last Friday. How do you explain that to an old man? That's been the most difficult thing of all, getting used to death.

Pause. Buzzer and light in number fifteen. The WOMAN leaves. The panel fills with buzzers and lights.

8

In the park. The SHORT WOMAN is seated on a bench. She opens her bag and scatters food for the pigeons. It is not clear what sort of food it is: not pieces of bread. The WOMAN lights a cigarette; she smokes as she watches the pigeons eat.

TALL MAN: Do you mind?

He points to the bench. She barely shakes her head. The TALL MAN sits down beside her. He is carrying a newspaper. The SHORT WOMAN extinguishes her cigarette.

I love the mornings. The city seems different in the mornings.

Silence.

A lot of people hate the idea of working nights. But everything has its good side. Like having your mornings free. The streets are the same, but the city seems totally different. People's faces are different. Different type of people about. People who feed birds. I've always liked people who feed birds or wild cats. It's selfless. They don't expect anything in return.

SHORT WOMAN: I don't like cats.

TALL MAN: I mean it says something good about them. I don't understand why people are cruel to animals. I don't understand cruelty.

SHORT WOMAN: I only bring the pigeons leftovers. So as not to have to throw them out.

TALL MAN: There are people who do good things without expecting anything in return. Your husband. We should all be grateful to him. He makes everyone's lives easier without asking anything in return. The little things that make everyone's lives easier. Like fixing the lamp in the front doorway...not just any old lamp.

SHORT WOMAN: My husband's good with his hands.

TALL MAN: Oh I know. He can't bear to see anything broken. He'd like the world to be perfect. Everything matters to him, the tiniest detail. That's why it's so easy to disappoint him. It's hard to meet other people's expectations of us. He hates you smoking. Don't worry, I won't say anything, your secret's safe with me.

SHORT WOMAN: He doesn't like the smell of tobacco. He doesn't mind outside. I don't think he minds.

TALL MAN: I always see you with your cigarette, with the pigeons at your feet. I cut through the park when I'm going for the paper. At different times of the day. I don't have an alarm clock. When I'm at work, I sometimes get some sleep, so a couple of hours at home does me. Whether I get up at ten or one, there you are, sitting on this bench.

SHORT WOMAN: A lot of people don't like the smell of tobacco.

TALL MAN: No, I know. It's the same at work. The smell hangs in the air for hours. What can you do, though? Everyone smokes where I work. Do you know what I do?

SHORT WOMAN: No.

TALL MAN: Does your husband not talk to you about me?

Silence. The WOMAN stands up.

SHORT WOMAN: I sit for a while to look at the pigeons. On my way to the shops. I stop because I've always got a bit of time. And not too much to get in. He does the big shop every Saturday morning. He always knows where to get the best bargains. All I really get is the bread. To tell you the truth, I'm lucky. He does the shopping, the cooking, the cleaning. I've a lot of time for myself.

She is about to go.

TALL MAN: The programme last night was very interesting. That man whose family knew nothing about him.

The WOMAN stops.

The doctor was very good. 'We all have secrets. We all have something to hide. That's why we don't trust other people. Don't be ashamed of your secret. It's feeling ashamed that's preventing you from sleeping'.

Silence. The WOMAN sits down.

There's a television at work. A small one, just to kill time. A couple of weeks ago I tuned into that programme, the one you like. Very interesting. Your husband makes fun of it, but that man, the doctor, I think he knows what he's talking about. Maybe his explanations are a bit on the outlandish side, but what does that matter as long as he helps people to feel better. Perhaps he can cure people, who knows? Who can tell why someone can't sleep? And the questions he asks make sense? 'Do you spend a lot of time on your own?' 'Why do you not have children?' 'When was the last time your husband touched you?'

Silence.

SHORT WOMAN: He must be thinking about something. He forgot his brother's birthday, he never forgets dates. He leaves the lights on. He doesn't sleep like he used to, and he goes to bed without dinner. Something must be worrying him, and he doesn't want to tell me. It might be something at work. Has he said anything to you? People don't give him his due. Or maybe it's my fault. I'm a bit awkward. We used to go out with other couples, but I always ended up doing or saying something. He worries about me. He's always watching out for me. Perhaps if I went back to work… They told me I could go back whenever I wanted. I try and do things the way he likes them. I didn't watch any telly today. He gave me a novel, but the truth is it's hard going. I get sleepy. My sleeping patterns have changed. I take tablets, but they give me headaches and I don't know what else they might be doing to me. Did you see the programme with that man who didn't know whether he was sleeping or not? I've only twenty pages to go. I will get through it.

She is about to go. The MAN's voice stops her.

TALL MAN: He phoned me at work last night. He told me not to go in today...a man who never misses a day himself. It's his birthday and he wants to do something special tonight. He hasn't said how we're going to celebrate. All he's told me is what he wants for a present.

Silence.

SHORT WOMAN: What can I do?

9

The SHORT MAN is silently consulting a computer. He lifts the phone. He speaks at the same time as he searches for information on the computer.

SHORT MAN: Good morning, could I speak to the owner of the property listed on the land register as L-5393959?... Yes, that's the address... An irregularity in your registration has just come to light. The property is described as type D-3. But in fact it's an E-3. With that square footage, it's an E-3. Which implies a difference in your favour. Quite a considerable difference, because the rate is applied at 18 per cent rather than 22… I need a few details to amend the registration. How many people live in the property? How many in employment? Any invalid or chronically ill persons? Fine. An inspector will call out soon to check the dimensions of the property. As for the refund, how would you prefer to receive it?

The SHORT WOMAN comes in, saying goodbye to the unseen person who has brought her there.

SHORT WOMAN: I see him, thank you.

SHORT MAN: (*Into the phone.*) Excuse me, I'll phone you right back. (*He hangs up.*) What's wrong?

Silence. The WOMAN tries to talk to him, but speaks with difficulty.

SHORT WOMAN: It's very bright. I don't know why, I thought it would be darker. I didn't imagine it would look like this. With the window. The man who brought me here seemed very nice.

Silence.

SHORT MAN: What are you doing here?

Silence.

SHORT WOMAN: It's your birthday.

SHORT MAN: You've come to wish me happy birthday?

Silence. The WOMAN sits down on the other side of the table.

Has anything happened?

SHORT WOMAN: You're going to think this is funny.

SHORT MAN: Think what's funny?

Silence. The WOMAN tries to speak, but only manages to with an effort.

SHORT WOMAN: I was watching the telly and I suddenly felt very worried. I was watching one of those talk shows…

SHORT MAN: I'll be finished in an hour. Can you not hang on?

SHORT WOMAN: I don't know what the topic was. But they started saying awful things about foreigners. Awful people saying awful things. I felt really angry. I thought we should do something.

SHORT MAN: Yes. You're right.

SHORT WOMAN: Show them we care at least. At least show the ones who live nearby we care.

SHORT MAN: Yes.

SHORT WOMAN: Then that neighbour came into my head. Your friend. You know the one. He works nights. I can't get him out of my mind. His situation.

SHORT MAN: His situation?

SHORT WOMAN: You mean a lot to him. You can tell you're the only friend he's got here.

SHORT MAN: I don't understand what you mean. Are you saying he's…? What makes you think that? Because he works nights? He's no more foreign than you or me. He's got his own views on immigrants, and not very nice ones at that. Have you listened to the way he talks? I wish I could talk half as well as he does.

SHORT WOMAN: No, I know. He does talk very well, you can tell he's educated. It's hard to believe that a man like that should be at the beck and call of just anyone. Because he's got no papers. Do you know that according to that law, what's it called, the Immigration Act, do you know that all I have to do is lift the phone and he's in real trouble. I could have him expelled. I could make up something, that he'd assaulted me, anything. His word against mine. Do you think they'd believe the word of an illegal immigrant? It must be terrible living like that, people looking down on you. That's why I thought we should show them we care. You're going to think this is funny.

Silence.

I thought we could invite him to your birthday. Him and his wife, although she's started to be quite unpleasant. Does she say hello to you? He's much nicer. I would never have imagined he's foreign, if he hadn't told me. And that's when I understood. Because I'd been wondering about it. How could a man like that spend so much time with a man like you?

Silence. The WOMAN takes out a cigarette. She plays with it.

You're all on top of each other…in these offices. What happens if one day one of you feels like shouting out loud? What do you do if you feel like shouting? Go to the toilets? I've never heard you shout though. You never lose control. You know how to wait. That's something

71

I've learned from you: how to wait. You see, all these years, and I have learned something.

She lights the cigarette. Silence.

Why don't you shout? It's your birthday. Break the rules for once.

She draws deeply. She blows out smoke.

I'm not leaving the house. Nobody is going to make me give up my home.

Silence. She continues to smoke. The man lifts the phone and dials.

SHORT MAN: Sorry about that. Our system went down. We were…yes, that's right…how do you want the money to be paid?… Can you give me an account number?… Let me read that back. (*He reads out what he has written into the computer.*) 63458128… A couple of days at the most. Not at all, it's our job… We'll phone to arrange the inspection. Goodbye.

He hangs up. Pause.

I can hear hatred in your voice. And that hurts. But deep down I know you're right. You'll think this is funny, but the other day I thought: what would happen if, after all these years, she met somebody else. No, don't laugh: it could happen to anyone. I thought: how can I ask her not to meet somebody else? I know what you must be feeling. It's not your fault, or mine. I know that feeling. Take a look at this.

He opens a document on the computer, and invites her to read it. She does.

SHORT WOMAN: 'List of things I want to do that I can't do with her.'

She reads on in silence.

You never asked me to go to the zoo with you. We've done a lot of things together. We've gone to the cinema, we've…

SHORT MAN: It's the things we don't do that count, do you not think? As I was listening to you, I realised you could make a list like that too. I'm sure you have things you would like to have done. All the hugs I never gave you. All the dancing you missed out on… It suddenly occurred to me the other day: what if, after all these years, she was to meet somebody else?

Silence.

It's all I've been able to give you. I tried to look after you, but I can see it's not enough. You don't need to be looked after any more. I'll leave tomorrow, if you want. And tonight we'll celebrate my birthday with them, of course we will. We have to help people like that.

Pause. She extinguishes her cigarette. He hugs her.

I've been neglecting you recently, haven't I? Only thinking about myself. But did you think I would stop looking after you? Don't be silly: I won't stop looking after you. I'll keep on looking after you, if you want me to.

73

10

The SHORT WOMAN is sitting on the park bench. Night time. She is speaking into her mobile phone.

SHORT WOMAN: Doctor, hello… I'm phoning to tell you I'm not going to call any more, because I can sleep now… Yes, yes… I did everything you said, but that wasn't it. I cured myself. You're not capable of curing anyone. You don't understand anything. You're a fool. No, I don't have time. I'm going to bed.

She hangs up, but doesn't move. In the upstairs flat, the SHORT MAN and the TALL MAN are seated at a table laid for four, but at which only they seem to have eaten. The SHORT MAN closes his eyes, makes a wish, and blows out the candles on the cake; he signals to the TALL MAN, who gives him a present; the SHORT MAN unwraps it: a very fine notebook and a fountain pen; he strokes the notebook, flicks through its blank pages; takes the top off the fountain pen.

SHORT MAN: I don't know where to begin. I've been wanting this for so long and now the moment has come, I can't find the words. I'd like to begin there, with that feeling of not being able to find the words.

He puts the notebook and the fountain pen in front of the TALL MAN.

TALL MAN: 'Morning'. 'Morning'. Remember? Two shadows passing every night on the stairs. That's all we were. Two shadows. But we've changed, haven't we? We've shared important moments, decisive moments. You've taught me a lot, and I know you've learned from me. Neither of us would have got as far if we hadn't have come together. But there comes a time, you know it as well as I do, we've both known it right from the start, there comes a time when you have to go on alone. Like that animal you told me about that followed the moon one night into the woods on its own. Or the young prince who while everybody else was sleeping crept out of the palace and went naked into the woods, on his own.

He puts the notebook and fountain pen in front of the SHORT MAN. He stands to go.

SHORT MAN: So you're saying goodbye? You're turning my birthday party into a final goodbye? All right, go…now…go wherever you want. I won't follow you. I've spent the whole day thinking I might have been wrong about you. You told me that 'The Hedgehog and the Fox' was from the 'Arabian Nights'. But it's not. It's not an Arabian story. It's Greek. Did I make a mistake when I chose you? Perhaps it shouldn't have been you I chose.

He lifts a figure from the train set. A woman with a suitcase.

I've been thinking about your wife. I've not been able to get her out of my mind. There's something otherworldly about her. I want to take her to the zoo. To the nocturnals enclosure.

The SHORT MAN produces a bottle of wine. It is the same wine as the one they toasted with that first day in the 'Jakarta'. He fills his own glass. He tosses the figure into the TALL MAN's glass and then fills it with wine.

I said you can go. What's keeping you?

Pause. The TALL MAN goes back to his chair. He opens the notebook, flicks through its blank pages. He picks up the fountain pen. The TALL WOMAN walks to the park and stops in front of the SHORT WOMAN.

TALL WOMAN: Are you not cold? You should go home.

Silence.

Don't just sit there. You'll freeze.

Silence.

I'm sorry, I can't stay with you. I'm meeting someone. At the station. I've a train to catch.

Silence.

I know it's a cliché, but I never thought it would happen to me. You love someone, you think you're going to be with them the rest of your life, and suddenly somebody else comes along. Do you think I should feel guilty? Tomorrow morning he'll wake up, and I won't be there. But he'll get by, he'll get by without me.

Silence.

Do you think it's crazy? I hardly know him, I just know I like being with him. I don't even know where he's taking me. I have to wait on the platform until he waves his hat at me, out of a window on one of the trains. That's the signal. His hat. And that's the train I catch.

Silence.

Why don't you come with me? He won't
mind. He's such fun to be with. Come
with us. As long as you don't mind not
knowing where the train's going.

*The SHORT WOMAN stands up. She walks
towards her home. The TALL WOMAN watches
her walk away and heads towards the station.
The TALL MAN is writing. The men do not react
to the entrance of the SHORT WOMAN.*

SHORT MAN: I was even going to phone in sick.
The fact is I didn't speak to anyone all
morning. You know what I think about
the people at work.

The TALL MAN writes.

I walked home. Like I told you. The
feeling of revenge.

The TALL MAN writes.

In the kitchen. What it means to cook.
Like a new start.

The TALL MAN writes.

The train.

The TALL MAN writes.

The presents.

*The TALL MAN writes. Full stop. The TALL
MAN hands the notebook to the SHORT MAN.
The SHORT MAN reads aloud what is written
there.*

'Trembling at the first word. Years from
now the words I write down here will
give me back the secret of this moment,
its deepest meaning'. (*Silence.*) On this
long-awaited day, I was tempted to turn

my back on my duties, so as not to have
to mix with those people whose mere
presence leaves a bitterness in my soul.
I walked home, through places where
my illusions had been stolen from me,
illusions that it's now time to recapture.
Suddenly I saw the city as jungle in
which only one creature may triumph: a
creature that is part hedgehog, part fox.
As though it were some ritual of renewal,
I devoted the afternoon to preparing the
first banquet of my new life. And as I
savoured it, I thought 'A good dish, like a
good life, is a question of balance'. When
evening fell, I inaugurated the train,
which cut through the night like a star.
But the miracle was still to happen. When
I opened the presents, it did. I felt it at
last, in my heart, at last. Happiness.'

Silence. He makes a gesture of approval.

You can go and rest. See you tomorrow.

*The TALL MAN makes to leave. He is stopped by
the voice of the SHORT WOMAN.*

SHORT WOMAN: I want to dance.

Pause.

SHORT MAN: (*To the TALL MAN.*) You heard. She
wants to dance. She's been thinking
about you lately. But don't worry. You
know I wouldn't let anybody hurt you.
She won't ask for anything ugly, or
degrading, nothing humiliating. (*To the
SHORT WOMAN.*) If you're going to put
music on, make sure it doesn't annoy the
neighbours.

Happily, he re-reads the opening sentences of his diary. He presses a switch and the night-train starts up. The SHORT WOMAN puts her hands on the TALL MAN and makes him dance. The TALL WOMAN watches as her train pulls in.